THIS BOOK

BELONGS TO

Adventure

AWAITS

# OUTDOOR ESSENTIALS

consider carrying
an external battery
charger

Always pack
extra food.

be lightweight and
minimal on a
backpacking

Consider taking
First Aid and
medications

## TRIP LOCATION

## CHECKLIST

## DATE

## MILEAGE

| START | ENDING |
|-------|--------|
|       |        |

TOTAL MILES TRAVELLED

## ACTIVIES PLAN AT TRIP

- ⭘ HIKING
- ⭘ FISHING
- ⭘ CANOEING
- ⭘ HOTTUB
- ⭘ BOAT

- ⭘ SPORTS
- ⭘ CYCLING
- ⭘ SITE SEEING
- ⭘
- ⭘

- ⭘
- ⭘
- ⭘
- ⭘
- ⭘

## WEATHER ON SITE

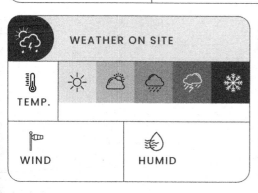

TEMP.

WIND

HUMID

## COST

| TRANSPORT | PACKAGING |
|-----------|-----------|
| FOOD      | OTHER     |

1

## CAMPGROUND DETAILS

| LOCATION | DURATION |
| --- | --- |

**ADDRESS**

| PHONE | WEB |
| --- | --- |

| PRICE | RATING ☆☆☆☆☆ |
| --- | --- |

☆☆☆☆☆     ☆☆☆☆☆     ☆☆☆☆☆

**CLEANLINESS**     **WATER**     **NOISE**

## TRIP HIGHLIGHTS / MEMORIES

## TRIP LOCATION

### CHECKLIST

### DATE

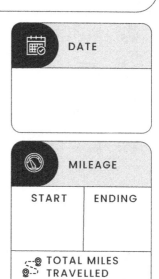

### MILEAGE

| START | ENDING |
|-------|--------|
|       |        |

TOTAL MILES TRAVELLED

### ACTIVIES PLAN AT TRIP

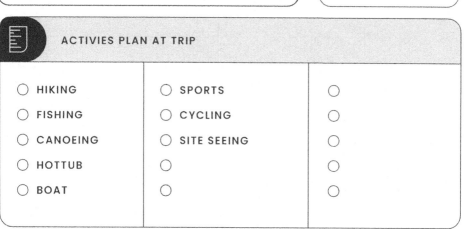

- ◯ HIKING
- ◯ FISHING
- ◯ CANOEING
- ◯ HOTTUB
- ◯ BOAT

- ◯ SPORTS
- ◯ CYCLING
- ◯ SITE SEEING
- ◯
- ◯

- ◯
- ◯
- ◯
- ◯
- ◯

### WEATHER ON SITE

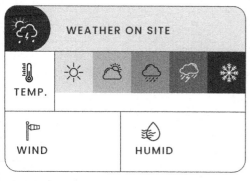

TEMP.

WIND

HUMID

### COST

| TRANSPORT | PACKAGING |
|-----------|-----------|
| FOOD      | OTHER     |

## CAMPGROUND DETAILS

**LOCATION**

**DURATION**

**ADDRESS**

**PHONE**

**WEB**

**PRICE**

**RATING** ☆☆☆☆☆

☆☆☆☆☆
**CLEANLINESS**

☆☆☆☆☆
**WATER**

☆☆☆☆☆
**NOISE**

## TRIP HIGHLIGHTS / MEMORIES

## TRIP LOCATION

## CHECKLIST

## DATE

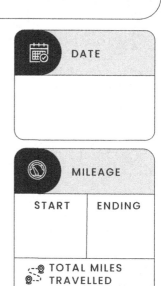

## MILEAGE

| START | ENDING |
|-------|--------|

TOTAL MILES TRAVELLED

## ACTIVIES PLAN AT TRIP

| | | |
|---|---|---|
| ○ HIKING | ○ SPORTS | ○ |
| ○ FISHING | ○ CYCLING | ○ |
| ○ CANOEING | ○ SITE SEEING | ○ |
| ○ HOTTUB | ○ | ○ |
| ○ BOAT | ○ | ○ |

## WEATHER ON SITE

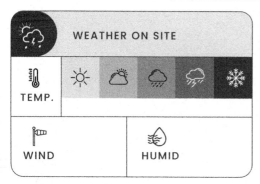

TEMP.

WIND

HUMID

## COST

| TRANSPORT | PACKAGING |
|-----------|-----------|
| FOOD | OTHER |

1

## CAMPGROUND DETAILS

**LOCATION**

**DURATION**

**ADDRESS**

**PHONE**

**WEB**

**PRICE**

**RATING** ☆☆☆☆☆

☆☆☆☆☆
**CLEANLINESS**

☆☆☆☆☆
**WATER**

☆☆☆☆☆
**NOISE**

## TRIP HIGHLIGHTS / MEMORIES

## TRIP LOCATION

### CHECKLIST

### DATE

### MILEAGE

| START | ENDING |
|-------|--------|

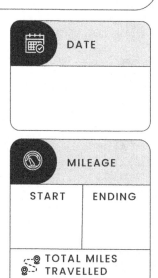

TOTAL MILES
TRAVELLED

### ACTIVIES PLAN AT TRIP

- ○ HIKING
- ○ FISHING
- ○ CANOEING
- ○ HOTTUB
- ○ BOAT

- ○ SPORTS
- ○ CYCLING
- ○ SITE SEEING
- ○
- ○

- ○
- ○
- ○
- ○
- ○

### WEATHER ON SITE

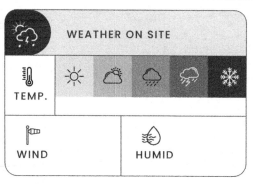

TEMP.

WIND

HUMID

### COST

| TRANSPORT | PACKAGING |
|-----------|-----------|
| FOOD | OTHER |

## CAMPGROUND DETAILS

| LOCATION | DURATION |
|---|---|

| ADDRESS | |

| PHONE | WEB |

| PRICE | RATING ☆☆☆☆☆ |

| ☆☆☆☆☆ | ☆☆☆☆☆ | ☆☆☆☆☆ |
|---|---|---|
| CLEANLINESS | WATER | NOISE |

## TRIP HIGHLIGHTS / MEMORIES

------------------------------------------------

------------------------------------------------

------------------------------------------------

------------------------------------------------

------------------------------------------------

------------------------------------------------

------------------------------------------------

------------------------------------------------

------------------------------------------------

------------------------------------------------

------------------------------------------------

------------------------------------------------

------------------------------------------------

------------------------------------------------

## TRIP LOCATION

## CHECKLIST

## DATE

## MILEAGE

| START | ENDING |
|-------|--------|
|       |        |

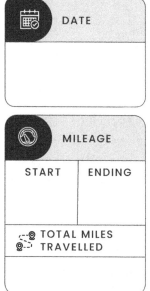 TOTAL MILES TRAVELLED

## ACTIVIES PLAN AT TRIP

- ◯ HIKING
- ◯ FISHING
- ◯ CANOEING
- ◯ HOTTUB
- ◯ BOAT

- ◯ SPORTS
- ◯ CYCLING
- ◯ SITE SEEING
- ◯
- ◯

- ◯
- ◯
- ◯
- ◯
- ◯

## WEATHER ON SITE

| TEMP. | ☀ | ⛅ | 🌧 | ⛈ | ❄ |
|-------|---|---|---|---|---|

WIND

HUMID

## COST

|           | PACKAGING |
|-----------|-----------|
| TRANSPORT | PACKAGING |
| FOOD      | OTHER     |

## CAMPGROUND DETAILS

| LOCATION | DURATION |
|----------|----------|
| ADDRESS | |
| PHONE | WEB |
| PRICE | RATING ☆☆☆☆☆ |

☆☆☆☆☆
**CLEANLINESS**

☆☆☆☆☆
**WATER**

☆☆☆☆☆
**NOISE**

## TRIP HIGHLIGHTS / MEMORIES

# 🏕️ TRIP LOCATION

## 📋 CHECKLIST

---
---
---
---
---
---
---

## 📅 DATE

## 🕐 MILEAGE

| START | ENDING |
|-------|--------|
|       |        |

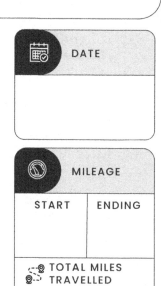
**TOTAL MILES TRAVELLED**

## 📋 ACTIVIES PLAN AT TRIP

| | | |
|---|---|---|
| ○ HIKING | ○ SPORTS | ○ |
| ○ FISHING | ○ CYCLING | ○ |
| ○ CANOEING | ○ SITE SEEING | ○ |
| ○ HOTTUB | ○ | ○ |
| ○ BOAT | ○ | ○ |

## 🌧️ WEATHER ON SITE

| 🌡️ TEMP. | ☀️ ⛅ 🌧️ ⛈️ ❄️ |
|-----------|-----------------|
| 💨 WIND | 💧 HUMID |

## 💵 COST

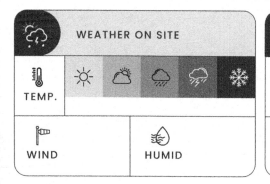

| TRANSPORT | PACKAGING |
|-----------|-----------|
| FOOD | OTHER |

## CAMPGROUND DETAILS

| LOCATION | DURATION |
|---|---|

**ADDRESS**

| PHONE | WEB |
|---|---|

| PRICE | RATING ☆☆☆☆☆ |
|---|---|

| ☆☆☆☆☆ | ☆☆☆☆☆ | ☆☆☆☆☆ |
|---|---|---|
| CLEANLINESS | WATER | NOISE |

## TRIP HIGHLIGHTS / MEMORIES

## 🏕 TRIP LOCATION

### 📝 CHECKLIST

### 📅 DATE

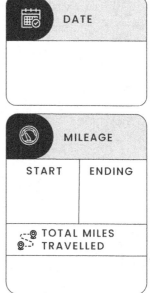

### 🧭 MILEAGE

| START | ENDING |
|-------|--------|
|       |        |

📍 TOTAL MILES
TRAVELLED

### 📝 ACTIVIES PLAN AT TRIP

- ◯ HIKING
- ◯ FISHING
- ◯ CANOEING
- ◯ HOTTUB
- ◯ BOAT

- ◯ SPORTS
- ◯ CYCLING
- ◯ SITE SEEING
- ◯
- ◯

- ◯
- ◯
- ◯
- ◯
- ◯

### 🌧 WEATHER ON SITE

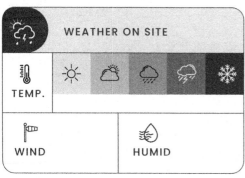

🌡 TEMP. | ☀ 🌤 🌧 ⛈ ❄

🎐 WIND | 💧 HUMID

### 💵 COST

|            |           |
|------------|-----------|
| TRANSPORT  | PACKAGING |
|            |           |
| FOOD       | OTHER     |

## CAMPGROUND DETAILS

LOCATION                    DURATION

ADDRESS

PHONE                       WEB

PRICE                       RATING ☆☆☆☆☆

☆☆☆☆☆          ☆☆☆☆☆          ☆☆☆☆☆
CLEANLINESS        WATER              NOISE

## TRIP HIGHLIGHTS / MEMORIES

## TRIP LOCATION

### CHECKLIST

### DATE

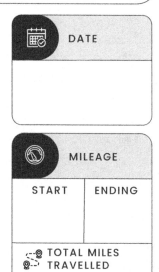

### MILEAGE

| START | ENDING |
|-------|--------|
|       |        |

TOTAL MILES TRAVELLED

### ACTIVIES PLAN AT TRIP

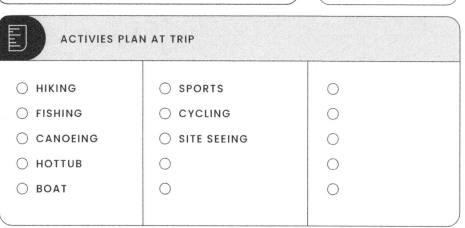

- ◯ HIKING
- ◯ FISHING
- ◯ CANOEING
- ◯ HOTTUB
- ◯ BOAT

- ◯ SPORTS
- ◯ CYCLING
- ◯ SITE SEEING
- ◯
- ◯

- ◯
- ◯
- ◯
- ◯
- ◯

### WEATHER ON SITE

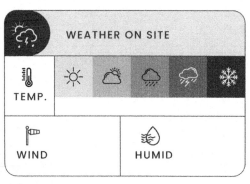

TEMP.

WIND

HUMID

### COST

| TRANSPORT | PACKAGING |
|-----------|-----------|
| FOOD      | OTHER     |

## CAMPGROUND DETAILS

**LOCATION**

**DURATION**

**ADDRESS**

**PHONE**

**WEB**

**PRICE**

**RATING** ☆☆☆☆☆

☆☆☆☆☆
CLEANLINESS

☆☆☆☆☆
WATER

☆☆☆☆☆
NOISE

## TRIP HIGHLIGHTS / MEMORIES

# TRIP LOCATION

## CHECKLIST

## DATE

## MILEAGE

| START | ENDING |
|-------|--------|
|       |        |

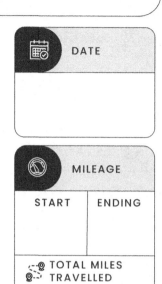

TOTAL MILES
TRAVELLED

## ACTIVIES PLAN AT TRIP

- ◯ HIKING
- ◯ FISHING
- ◯ CANOEING
- ◯ HOTTUB
- ◯ BOAT

- ◯ SPORTS
- ◯ CYCLING
- ◯ SITE SEEING
- ◯
- ◯

- ◯
- ◯
- ◯
- ◯
- ◯

## WEATHER ON SITE

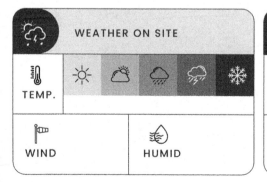

| TEMP. | ☀ | ⛅ | 🌧 | ⛈ | ❄ |
|-------|---|---|---|---|---|

| WIND | HUMID |
|------|-------|

## COST

|           |           |
|-----------|-----------|
| TRANSPORT | PACKAGING |
| FOOD      | OTHER     |

## CAMPGROUND DETAILS

LOCATION

DURATION

ADDRESS

PHONE

WEB

PRICE

RATING ☆☆☆☆☆

☆☆☆☆☆
CLEANLINESS

☆☆☆☆☆
WATER

☆☆☆☆☆
NOISE

## TRIP HIGHLIGHTS / MEMORIES

## TRIP LOCATION

## CHECKLIST

## DATE

## MILEAGE

| START | ENDING |
|-------|--------|

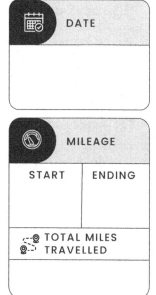

| TOTAL MILES TRAVELLED | |
|-----------------------|--|

## ACTIVIES PLAN AT TRIP

- ◯ HIKING
- ◯ FISHING
- ◯ CANOEING
- ◯ HOTTUB
- ◯ BOAT

- ◯ SPORTS
- ◯ CYCLING
- ◯ SITE SEEING
- ◯
- ◯

- ◯
- ◯
- ◯
- ◯
- ◯

## WEATHER ON SITE

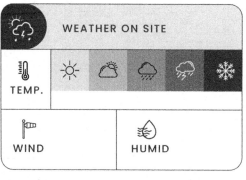

| TEMP. | ☀ | ⛅ | 🌧 | ⛈ | ❄ |
|-------|---|---|---|---|---|
| WIND | | HUMID | | | |

## COST

| TRANSPORT | PACKAGING |
|-----------|-----------|
| FOOD | OTHER |

## CAMPGROUND DETAILS

| | |
|---|---|
| LOCATION | DURATION |
| ADDRESS | |
| PHONE | WEB |
| PRICE | RATING ☆☆☆☆☆ |

☆☆☆☆☆
**CLEANLINESS**

☆☆☆☆☆
**WATER**

☆☆☆☆☆
**NOISE**

## TRIP HIGHLIGHTS / MEMORIES

---
---
---
---
---
---
---
---
---
---
---
---
---
---

## TRIP LOCATION

## CHECKLIST

## DATE

## MILEAGE

| START | ENDING |
|-------|--------|

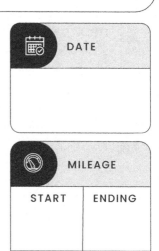 TOTAL MILES TRAVELLED

## ACTIVIES PLAN AT TRIP

- ○ HIKING
- ○ FISHING
- ○ CANOEING
- ○ HOTTUB
- ○ BOAT

- ○ SPORTS
- ○ CYCLING
- ○ SITE SEEING
- ○
- ○

- ○
- ○
- ○
- ○
- ○

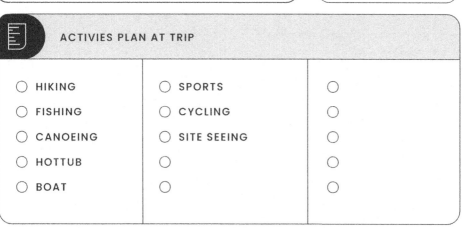

## WEATHER ON SITE

TEMP.

WIND

HUMID

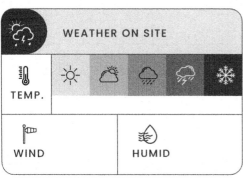

## COST

| TRANSPORT | PACKAGING |
|-----------|-----------|
| FOOD | OTHER |

## CAMPGROUND DETAILS

| | |
|---|---|
| 🏕️ LOCATION | 🕐 DURATION |
| 📍 ADDRESS | |
| 📞 PHONE | 🌐 WEB |
| 💵 PRICE | 🤚 RATING ☆☆☆☆☆ |

☆☆☆☆☆
**CLEANLINESS**

☆☆☆☆☆
**WATER**

☆☆☆☆☆
**NOISE**

## TRIP HIGHLIGHTS / MEMORIES

---

---

---

---

---

---

---

---

---

---

---

---

---

---

## TRIP LOCATION

### CHECKLIST

### DATE

### MILEAGE

| START | ENDING |
|-------|--------|
|       |        |

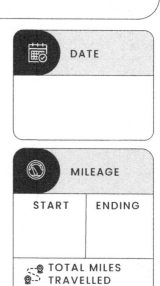 TOTAL MILES TRAVELLED

### ACTIVIES PLAN AT TRIP

| | | |
|---|---|---|
| ○ HIKING | ○ SPORTS | ○ |
| ○ FISHING | ○ CYCLING | ○ |
| ○ CANOEING | ○ SITE SEEING | ○ |
| ○ HOTTUB | ○ | ○ |
| ○ BOAT | ○ | ○ |

### WEATHER ON SITE

| TEMP. | ☀ | ⛅ | ☁ | ⛈ | ❄ |
|-------|---|---|---|---|---|

| WIND | HUMID |
|------|-------|

### COST

| TRANSPORT | PACKAGING |
|-----------|-----------|
| FOOD      | OTHER     |

## CAMPGROUND DETAILS

**LOCATION**

**DURATION**

**ADDRESS**

**PHONE**

**WEB**

**PRICE**

**RATING** ☆☆☆☆☆

☆☆☆☆☆
**CLEANLINESS**

☆☆☆☆☆
**WATER**

☆☆☆☆☆
**NOISE**

## TRIP HIGHLIGHTS / MEMORIES

## TRIP LOCATION

### CHECKLIST

### DATE

### MILEAGE

| START | ENDING |
|-------|--------|

TOTAL MILES TRAVELLED

### ACTIVIES PLAN AT TRIP

| | | |
|---|---|---|
| ○ HIKING | ○ SPORTS | ○ |
| ○ FISHING | ○ CYCLING | ○ |
| ○ CANOEING | ○ SITE SEEING | ○ |
| ○ HOTTUB | ○ | ○ |
| ○ BOAT | ○ | ○ |

### WEATHER ON SITE

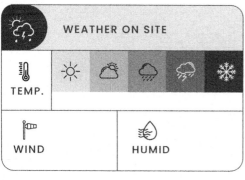

TEMP.

WIND     HUMID

### COST

| TRANSPORT | PACKAGING |
|-----------|-----------|
| FOOD | OTHER |

## CAMPGROUND DETAILS

**LOCATION**

**DURATION**

**ADDRESS**

**PHONE**

**WEB**

**PRICE**

**RATING** ☆☆☆☆☆

☆☆☆☆☆
**CLEANLINESS**

☆☆☆☆☆
**WATER**

☆☆☆☆☆
**NOISE**

## TRIP HIGHLIGHTS / MEMORIES

## TRIP LOCATION

## CHECKLIST

## DATE

## MILEAGE

| START | ENDING |
|-------|--------|

### TOTAL MILES TRAVELLED

## ACTIVIES PLAN AT TRIP

- ○ HIKING
- ○ FISHING
- ○ CANOEING
- ○ HOTTUB
- ○ BOAT

- ○ SPORTS
- ○ CYCLING
- ○ SITE SEEING
- ○
- ○

- ○
- ○
- ○
- ○
- ○

## WEATHER ON SITE

| TEMP. | | | | | |
|-------|---|---|---|---|---|

| WIND | HUMID |
|------|-------|

## COST

| TRANSPORT | PACKAGING |
|-----------|-----------|
| FOOD | OTHER |

## CAMPGROUND DETAILS

| | |
|---|---|
| **LOCATION** | **DURATION** |
| **ADDRESS** | |
| **PHONE** | **WEB** |
| **PRICE** | **RATING** ☆☆☆☆☆ |

☆☆☆☆☆
**CLEANLINESS**

☆☆☆☆☆
**WATER**

☆☆☆☆☆
**NOISE**

## TRIP HIGHLIGHTS / MEMORIES

## TRIP LOCATION

## CHECKLIST

## DATE

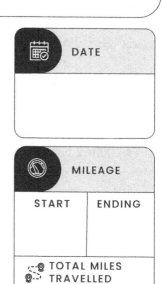

## MILEAGE

| START | ENDING |
|-------|--------|

**TOTAL MILES TRAVELLED**

## ACTIVIES PLAN AT TRIP

- ○ HIKING
- ○ FISHING
- ○ CANOEING
- ○ HOTTUB
- ○ BOAT

- ○ SPORTS
- ○ CYCLING
- ○ SITE SEEING
- ○
- ○

- ○
- ○
- ○
- ○
- ○

## WEATHER ON SITE

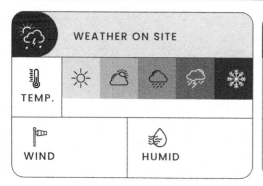

**TEMP.**

**WIND**

**HUMID**

## COST

| TRANSPORT | PACKAGING |
|-----------|-----------|
| FOOD | OTHER |

1

## CAMPGROUND DETAILS

| LOCATION | DURATION |
|---|---|

**ADDRESS**

| PHONE | WEB |
|---|---|

| PRICE | RATING ☆☆☆☆☆ |
|---|---|

☆☆☆☆☆     ☆☆☆☆☆     ☆☆☆☆☆

**CLEANLINESS**     **WATER**     **NOISE**

## TRIP HIGHLIGHTS / MEMORIES

## TRIP LOCATION

## CHECKLIST

## DATE

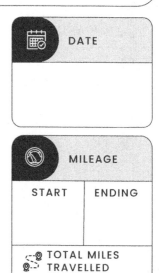

## MILEAGE

| START | ENDING |
|-------|--------|
|       |        |

TOTAL MILES
TRAVELLED

## ACTIVIES PLAN AT TRIP

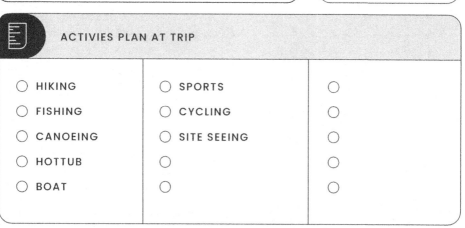

- ○ HIKING
- ○ FISHING
- ○ CANOEING
- ○ HOTTUB
- ○ BOAT

- ○ SPORTS
- ○ CYCLING
- ○ SITE SEEING
- ○
- ○

- ○
- ○
- ○
- ○
- ○

## WEATHER ON SITE

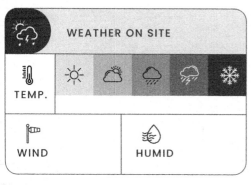

TEMP.

WIND

HUMID

## COST

| TRANSPORT | PACKAGING |
|-----------|-----------|
| FOOD      | OTHER     |

1

## CAMPGROUND DETAILS

| | |
|---|---|
| LOCATION | DURATION |
| ADDRESS | |
| PHONE | WEB |
| PRICE | RATING ☆☆☆☆☆ |

| ☆☆☆☆☆ | ☆☆☆☆☆ | ☆☆☆☆☆ |
|---|---|---|
| CLEANLINESS | WATER | NOISE |

## TRIP HIGHLIGHTS / MEMORIES

_____

_____

_____

_____

_____

_____

_____

_____

_____

_____

_____

_____

_____

_____

## TRIP LOCATION

## CHECKLIST

## DATE

## MILEAGE

| START | ENDING |
|-------|--------|
|       |        |

TOTAL MILES TRAVELLED

## ACTIVIES PLAN AT TRIP

| | | |
|---|---|---|
| ○ HIKING | ○ SPORTS | ○ |
| ○ FISHING | ○ CYCLING | ○ |
| ○ CANOEING | ○ SITE SEEING | ○ |
| ○ HOTTUB | ○ | ○ |
| ○ BOAT | ○ | ○ |

## WEATHER ON SITE

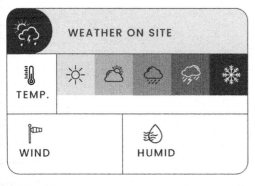

TEMP.

WIND          HUMID

## COST

| TRANSPORT | PACKAGING |
|-----------|-----------|
| FOOD      | OTHER     |

## CAMPGROUND DETAILS

| LOCATION | DURATION |
|---|---|

| ADDRESS | |
|---|---|

| PHONE | WEB |
|---|---|

| PRICE | RATING ☆☆☆☆☆ |
|---|---|

| ☆☆☆☆☆ | ☆☆☆☆☆ | ☆☆☆☆☆ |
|---|---|---|
| CLEANLINESS | WATER | NOISE |

## TRIP HIGHLIGHTS / MEMORIES

# TRIP LOCATION

## CHECKLIST

## DATE

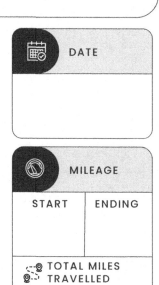

## MILEAGE

| START | ENDING |
|-------|--------|
|       |        |

### TOTAL MILES TRAVELLED

## ACTIVIES PLAN AT TRIP

| | | |
|---|---|---|
| ○ HIKING | ○ SPORTS | ○ |
| ○ FISHING | ○ CYCLING | ○ |
| ○ CANOEING | ○ SITE SEEING | ○ |
| ○ HOTTUB | ○ | ○ |
| ○ BOAT | ○ | ○ |

## WEATHER ON SITE

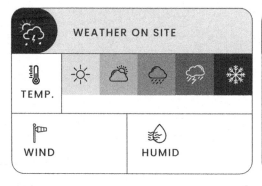

| TEMP. | ☼ | ⛅ | 🌧 | ⛈ | ❄ |
|-------|---|---|---|---|---|

| WIND | HUMID |
|------|-------|

## COST

| TRANSPORT | PACKAGING |
|-----------|-----------|
| FOOD | OTHER |

## CAMPGROUND DETAILS

| LOCATION | DURATION |
|----------|----------|
| ADDRESS | |
| PHONE | WEB |
| PRICE | RATING ☆☆☆☆☆ |

☆☆☆☆☆
**CLEANLINESS**

☆☆☆☆☆
**WATER**

☆☆☆☆☆
**NOISE**

## TRIP HIGHLIGHTS / MEMORIES

## TRIP LOCATION

## CHECKLIST

## DATE

## MILEAGE

| START | ENDING |
| --- | --- |
| | |

TOTAL MILES
TRAVELLED

## ACTIVIES PLAN AT TRIP

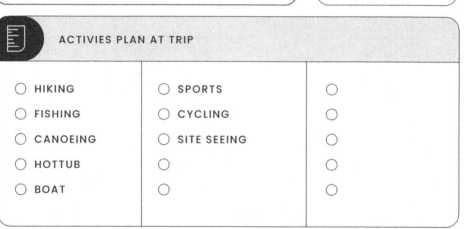

- ○ HIKING
- ○ FISHING
- ○ CANOEING
- ○ HOTTUB
- ○ BOAT
- ○ SPORTS
- ○ CYCLING
- ○ SITE SEEING
- ○
- ○
- ○
- ○
- ○
- ○
- ○

## WEATHER ON SITE

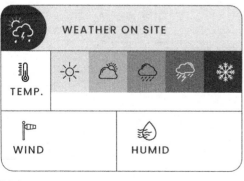

TEMP.

WIND    HUMID

## COST

| TRANSPORT | PACKAGING |
| --- | --- |
| FOOD | OTHER |

## CAMPGROUND DETAILS

| | |
|---|---|
| LOCATION | DURATION |
| ADDRESS | |
| PHONE | WEB |
| PRICE | RATING ☆☆☆☆☆ |

☆☆☆☆☆
**CLEANLINESS**

☆☆☆☆☆
**WATER**

☆☆☆☆☆
**NOISE**

## TRIP HIGHLIGHTS / MEMORIES

--------------------------------------------------
--------------------------------------------------
--------------------------------------------------
--------------------------------------------------
--------------------------------------------------
--------------------------------------------------
--------------------------------------------------
--------------------------------------------------
--------------------------------------------------
--------------------------------------------------
--------------------------------------------------
--------------------------------------------------
--------------------------------------------------
--------------------------------------------------

# TRIP LOCATION

## CHECKLIST

## DATE

## MILEAGE

| START | ENDING |
|-------|--------|
|       |        |

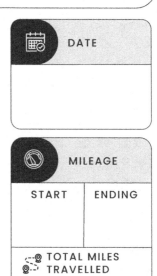 TOTAL MILES TRAVELLED

## ACTIVIES PLAN AT TRIP

| | | |
|---|---|---|
| ○ HIKING | ○ SPORTS | ○ |
| ○ FISHING | ○ CYCLING | ○ |
| ○ CANOEING | ○ SITE SEEING | ○ |
| ○ HOTTUB | ○ | ○ |
| ○ BOAT | ○ | ○ |

## WEATHER ON SITE

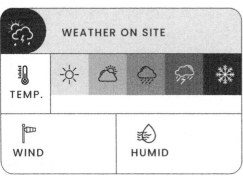

TEMP.

WIND

HUMID

## COST

| TRANSPORT | PACKAGING |
|-----------|-----------|
| FOOD | OTHER |

## CAMPGROUND DETAILS

| | |
|---|---|
| LOCATION | DURATION |
| ADDRESS | |
| PHONE | WEB |
| PRICE | RATING ☆☆☆☆☆ |

| ☆☆☆☆☆ | ☆☆☆☆☆ | ☆☆☆☆☆ |
|---|---|---|
| CLEANLINESS | WATER | NOISE |

## TRIP HIGHLIGHTS / MEMORIES

**TRIP LOCATION**

**CHECKLIST**

**DATE**

**MILEAGE**

| START | ENDING |
|-------|--------|

TOTAL MILES TRAVELLED

**ACTIVIES PLAN AT TRIP**

- ◯ HIKING
- ◯ FISHING
- ◯ CANOEING
- ◯ HOTTUB
- ◯ BOAT

- ◯ SPORTS
- ◯ CYCLING
- ◯ SITE SEEING
- ◯
- ◯

- ◯
- ◯
- ◯
- ◯
- ◯

**WEATHER ON SITE**

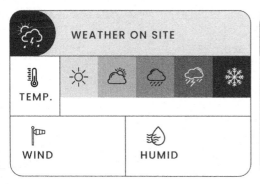

TEMP.

WIND

HUMID

**COST**

| TRANSPORT | PACKAGING |
|-----------|-----------|
| FOOD | OTHER |

## CAMPGROUND DETAILS

| LOCATION | DURATION |
|---|---|
| ADDRESS | |
| PHONE | WEB |
| PRICE | RATING ☆☆☆☆☆ |

☆☆☆☆☆
**CLEANLINESS**

☆☆☆☆☆
**WATER**

☆☆☆☆☆
**NOISE**

## TRIP HIGHLIGHTS / MEMORIES

## TRIP LOCATION

## CHECKLIST

## DATE

## MILEAGE

| START | ENDING |
|-------|--------|

TOTAL MILES TRAVELLED

## ACTIVIES PLAN AT TRIP

- ○ HIKING
- ○ FISHING
- ○ CANOEING
- ○ HOTTUB
- ○ BOAT

- ○ SPORTS
- ○ CYCLING
- ○ SITE SEEING
- ○
- ○

- ○
- ○
- ○
- ○
- ○

## WEATHER ON SITE

| TEMP. | ☀ ⛅ ☁ ⛈ ❄ |
|-------|-----------|
| WIND | HUMID |

## COST

| TRANSPORT | PACKAGING |
|-----------|-----------|
| FOOD | OTHER |

## CAMPGROUND DETAILS

| LOCATION | DURATION |
|---|---|
| ADDRESS | |
| PHONE | WEB |
| PRICE | RATING ☆☆☆☆☆ |

☆☆☆☆☆
**CLEANLINESS**

☆☆☆☆☆
**WATER**

☆☆☆☆☆
**NOISE**

## TRIP HIGHLIGHTS / MEMORIES

## TRIP LOCATION

## CHECKLIST

## DATE

## MILEAGE

| START | ENDING |
|-------|--------|
|       |        |

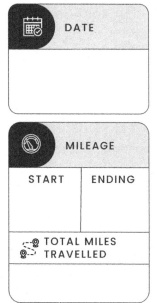 TOTAL MILES TRAVELLED

## ACTIVIES PLAN AT TRIP

- ○ HIKING
- ○ FISHING
- ○ CANOEING
- ○ HOTTUB
- ○ BOAT

- ○ SPORTS
- ○ CYCLING
- ○ SITE SEEING
- ○
- ○

- ○
- ○
- ○
- ○
- ○

## WEATHER ON SITE

| TEMP. | ☀ | ⛅ | ☁ | ⛈ | ❄ |
|-------|---|---|---|---|---|

| WIND | HUMID |
|------|-------|

## COST

| TRANSPORT | PACKAGING |
|-----------|-----------|
| FOOD      | OTHER     |

## CAMPGROUND DETAILS

**LOCATION**

**DURATION**

**ADDRESS**

**PHONE**

**WEB**

**PRICE**

**RATING** ☆☆☆☆☆

☆☆☆☆☆
CLEANLINESS

☆☆☆☆☆
WATER

☆☆☆☆☆
NOISE

## TRIP HIGHLIGHTS / MEMORIES

**TRIP LOCATION**

**CHECKLIST**

**DATE**

**MILEAGE**

| START | ENDING |
|-------|--------|

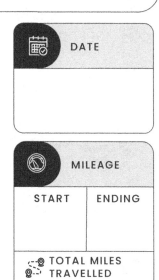 TOTAL MILES TRAVELLED

**ACTIVIES PLAN AT TRIP**

- ◯ HIKING
- ◯ FISHING
- ◯ CANOEING
- ◯ HOTTUB
- ◯ BOAT

- ◯ SPORTS
- ◯ CYCLING
- ◯ SITE SEEING
- ◯
- ◯

- ◯
- ◯
- ◯
- ◯
- ◯

**WEATHER ON SITE**

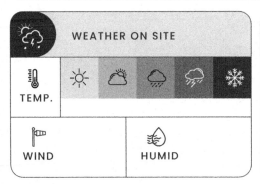

| TEMP. | ☀ | ⛅ | 🌧 | ⛈ | ❄ |
|-------|---|---|---|---|---|

| WIND | HUMID |
|------|-------|

**COST**

| TRANSPORT | PACKAGING |
|-----------|-----------|
| FOOD | OTHER |

1

## CAMPGROUND DETAILS

| | |
|---|---|
| LOCATION | DURATION |
| ADDRESS | |
| PHONE | WEB |
| PRICE | RATING ☆☆☆☆☆ |

| ☆☆☆☆☆ | ☆☆☆☆☆ | ☆☆☆☆☆ |
|---|---|---|
| CLEANLINESS | WATER | NOISE |

## TRIP HIGHLIGHTS / MEMORIES

# TRIP LOCATION

## CHECKLIST

## DATE

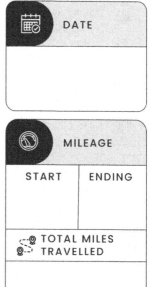

## MILEAGE

| START | ENDING |
|-------|--------|

TOTAL MILES TRAVELLED

## ACTIVIES PLAN AT TRIP

- ⭕ HIKING
- ⭕ FISHING
- ⭕ CANOEING
- ⭕ HOTTUB
- ⭕ BOAT

- ⭕ SPORTS
- ⭕ CYCLING
- ⭕ SITE SEEING
- ⭕
- ⭕

- ⭕
- ⭕
- ⭕
- ⭕
- ⭕

## WEATHER ON SITE

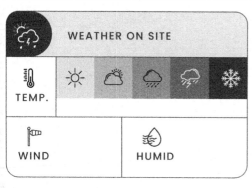

TEMP.

WIND    HUMID

## COST

| TRANSPORT | PACKAGING |
|-----------|-----------|
| FOOD | OTHER |

## CAMPGROUND DETAILS

**LOCATION**

**DURATION**

**ADDRESS**

**PHONE**

**WEB**

**PRICE**

**RATING** ☆☆☆☆☆

☆☆☆☆☆
**CLEANLINESS**

☆☆☆☆☆
**WATER**

☆☆☆☆☆
**NOISE**

## TRIP HIGHLIGHTS / MEMORIES

## TRIP LOCATION

### CHECKLIST

### DATE

### MILEAGE

| START | ENDING |
|-------|--------|

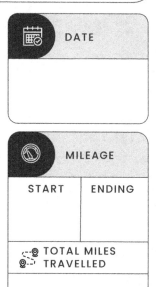

TOTAL MILES TRAVELLED

### ACTIVIES PLAN AT TRIP

- ○ HIKING
- ○ FISHING
- ○ CANOEING
- ○ HOTTUB
- ○ BOAT

- ○ SPORTS
- ○ CYCLING
- ○ SITE SEEING
- ○
- ○

- ○
- ○
- ○
- ○
- ○

### WEATHER ON SITE

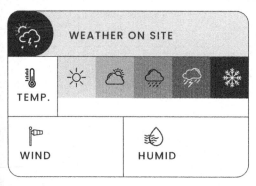

TEMP.

WIND

HUMID

### COST

| TRANSPORT | PACKAGING |
|-----------|-----------|
| FOOD | OTHER |

## CAMPGROUND DETAILS

| LOCATION | DURATION |
| --- | --- |
| ADDRESS | |
| PHONE | WEB |
| PRICE | RATING ☆☆☆☆☆ |

☆☆☆☆☆
CLEANLINESS

☆☆☆☆☆
WATER

☆☆☆☆☆
NOISE

## TRIP HIGHLIGHTS / MEMORIES

# TRIP LOCATION

## CHECKLIST

## DATE

## MILEAGE

| START | ENDING |
|-------|--------|
|       |        |

| 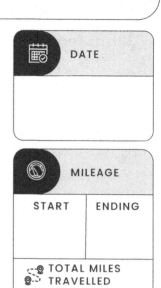 TOTAL MILES TRAVELLED | |

## ACTIVIES PLAN AT TRIP

| ○ HIKING | ○ SPORTS | ○ |
| ○ FISHING | ○ CYCLING | ○ |
| ○ CANOEING | ○ SITE SEEING | ○ |
| ○ HOTTUB | ○ | ○ |
| ○ BOAT | ○ | ○ |

## WEATHER ON SITE

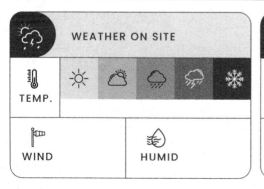

| TEMP. | ☀ | ⛅ | 🌧 | ⛈ | ❄ |
|-------|---|---|---|---|---|

| WIND | HUMID |

## COST

| TRANSPORT | PACKAGING |
|-----------|-----------|
| FOOD | OTHER |

## CAMPGROUND DETAILS

| | |
|---|---|
| LOCATION | DURATION |
| ADDRESS | |
| PHONE | WEB |
| PRICE | RATING ☆☆☆☆☆ |

☆☆☆☆☆
**CLEANLINESS**

☆☆☆☆☆
**WATER**

☆☆☆☆☆
**NOISE**

## TRIP HIGHLIGHTS / MEMORIES

# TRIP LOCATION

## CHECKLIST

## DATE

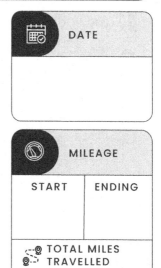

## MILEAGE

| START | ENDING |
|-------|--------|
|       |        |

TOTAL MILES TRAVELLED

## ACTIVIES PLAN AT TRIP

- ◯ HIKING
- ◯ FISHING
- ◯ CANOEING
- ◯ HOTTUB
- ◯ BOAT

- ◯ SPORTS
- ◯ CYCLING
- ◯ SITE SEEING
- ◯
- ◯

- ◯
- ◯
- ◯
- ◯
- ◯

## WEATHER ON SITE

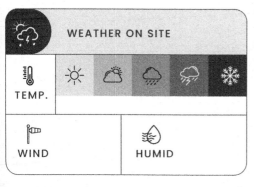

TEMP.

WIND

HUMID

## COST

| TRANSPORT | PACKAGING |
|-----------|-----------|
| FOOD      | OTHER     |

## CAMPGROUND DETAILS

| | | |
|---|---|---|
| **LOCATION** | | **DURATION** |
| **ADDRESS** | | |
| **PHONE** | | **WEB** |
| **PRICE** | | **RATING** ☆☆☆☆☆ |

☆☆☆☆☆     ☆☆☆☆☆     ☆☆☆☆☆

CLEANLINESS     WATER     NOISE

## TRIP HIGHLIGHTS / MEMORIES

_____

_____

_____

_____

_____

_____

_____

_____

_____

_____

_____

_____

_____

_____

## TRIP LOCATION

## CHECKLIST

## DATE

## MILEAGE

| START | ENDING |
|-------|--------|

TOTAL MILES TRAVELLED

## ACTIVIES PLAN AT TRIP

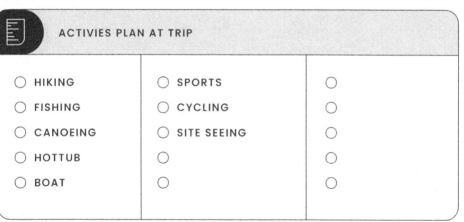

- ○ HIKING
- ○ FISHING
- ○ CANOEING
- ○ HOTTUB
- ○ BOAT

- ○ SPORTS
- ○ CYCLING
- ○ SITE SEEING
- ○
- ○

- ○
- ○
- ○
- ○
- ○

## WEATHER ON SITE

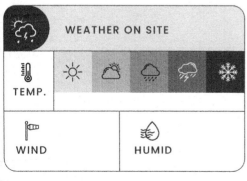

TEMP.

WIND

HUMID

## COST

| TRANSPORT | PACKAGING |
|-----------|-----------|
| FOOD | OTHER |

## CAMPGROUND DETAILS

| | |
|---|---|
| LOCATION | DURATION |
| ADDRESS | |
| PHONE | WEB |
| PRICE | RATING ☆☆☆☆☆ |

☆☆☆☆☆
CLEANLINESS

☆☆☆☆☆
WATER

☆☆☆☆☆
NOISE

## TRIP HIGHLIGHTS / MEMORIES

_____

_____

_____

_____

_____

_____

_____

_____

_____

_____

_____

_____

_____

## TRIP LOCATION

### CHECKLIST

### DATE

### MILEAGE

| START | ENDING |
|-------|--------|
|       |        |

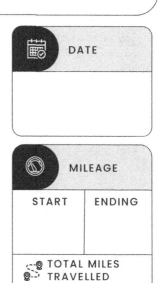 TOTAL MILES TRAVELLED

### ACTIVIES PLAN AT TRIP

| | | |
|---|---|---|
| ○ HIKING | ○ SPORTS | ○ |
| ○ FISHING | ○ CYCLING | ○ |
| ○ CANOEING | ○ SITE SEEING | ○ |
| ○ HOTTUB | ○ | ○ |
| ○ BOAT | ○ | ○ |

### WEATHER ON SITE

| TEMP. | ☀ | ⛅ | 🌧 | ⛈ | ❄ |
|-------|---|---|---|---|---|

| WIND | HUMID |
|------|-------|

### COST

| TRANSPORT | PACKAGING |
|-----------|-----------|
| FOOD | OTHER |

## CAMPGROUND DETAILS

| | | |
|---|---|---|
| LOCATION | | DURATION |
| ADDRESS | | |
| PHONE | | WEB |
| PRICE | | RATING ☆☆☆☆☆ |

☆☆☆☆☆
**CLEANLINESS**

☆☆☆☆☆
**WATER**

☆☆☆☆☆
**NOISE**

## TRIP HIGHLIGHTS / MEMORIES

_____

_____

_____

_____

_____

_____

_____

_____

_____

_____

_____

_____

_____

_____

## TRIP LOCATION

### CHECKLIST

### DATE

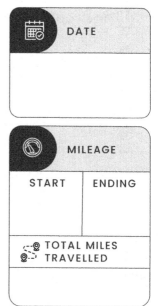

### MILEAGE

| START | ENDING |
|-------|--------|
|       |        |

🔗 **TOTAL MILES TRAVELLED**

### ACTIVIES PLAN AT TRIP

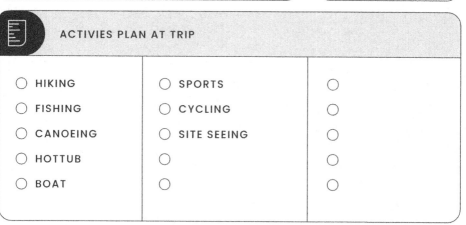

- ◯ HIKING
- ◯ FISHING
- ◯ CANOEING
- ◯ HOTTUB
- ◯ BOAT

- ◯ SPORTS
- ◯ CYCLING
- ◯ SITE SEEING
- ◯
- ◯

- ◯
- ◯
- ◯
- ◯
- ◯

### WEATHER ON SITE

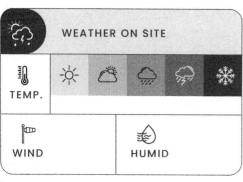

| TEMP. | ☀ | ⛅ | 🌧 | ⛈ | ❄ |
|-------|---|---|---|---|---|

| WIND | HUMID |
|------|-------|

### COST

| TRANSPORT | PACKAGING |
|-----------|-----------|
| FOOD | OTHER |

## CAMPGROUND DETAILS

| LOCATION | DURATION |
|---|---|
| ADDRESS | |
| PHONE | WEB |
| PRICE | RATING ☆☆☆☆☆ |

| ☆☆☆☆☆ | ☆☆☆☆☆ | ☆☆☆☆☆ |
|---|---|---|
| CLEANLINESS | WATER | NOISE |

## TRIP HIGHLIGHTS / MEMORIES

## TRIP LOCATION

## CHECKLIST

## DATE

## MILEAGE

| START | ENDING |
|-------|--------|
|       |        |

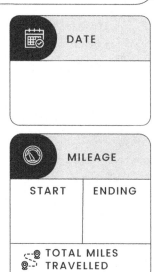 TOTAL MILES TRAVELLED

## ACTIVIES PLAN AT TRIP

| | | |
|---|---|---|
| ○ HIKING | ○ SPORTS | ○ |
| ○ FISHING | ○ CYCLING | ○ |
| ○ CANOEING | ○ SITE SEEING | ○ |
| ○ HOTTUB | ○ | ○ |
| ○ BOAT | ○ | ○ |

## WEATHER ON SITE

| TEMP. | | | | | |
|-------|---|---|---|---|---|

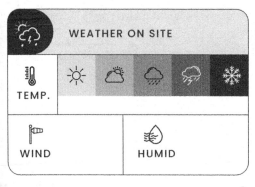

| WIND | HUMID |
|------|-------|

## COST

| TRANSPORT | PACKAGING |
|-----------|-----------|
| FOOD | OTHER |

## CAMPGROUND DETAILS

| | |
|---|---|
| LOCATION | DURATION |
| ADDRESS | |
| PHONE | WEB |
| PRICE | RATING ☆☆☆☆☆ |

| ☆☆☆☆☆ | ☆☆☆☆☆ | ☆☆☆☆☆ |
|---|---|---|
| CLEANLINESS | WATER | NOISE |

## TRIP HIGHLIGHTS / MEMORIES

_____

_____

_____

_____

_____

_____

_____

_____

_____

_____

_____

_____

_____

# TRIP LOCATION

## CHECKLIST

## DATE

## MILEAGE

| START | ENDING |
|-------|--------|

TOTAL MILES TRAVELLED

## ACTIVIES PLAN AT TRIP

- ○ HIKING
- ○ FISHING
- ○ CANOEING
- ○ HOTTUB
- ○ BOAT

- ○ SPORTS
- ○ CYCLING
- ○ SITE SEEING
- ○
- ○

- ○
- ○
- ○
- ○
- ○

## WEATHER ON SITE

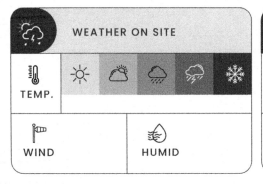

TEMP.

WIND

HUMID

## COST

| TRANSPORT | PACKAGING |
|-----------|-----------|
| FOOD | OTHER |

## CAMPGROUND DETAILS

**LOCATION**

**DURATION**

**ADDRESS**

**PHONE**

**WEB**

**PRICE**

**RATING** ☆☆☆☆☆

☆☆☆☆☆
**CLEANLINESS**

☆☆☆☆☆
**WATER**

☆☆☆☆☆
**NOISE**

## TRIP HIGHLIGHTS / MEMORIES

# TRIP LOCATION

## CHECKLIST

## DATE

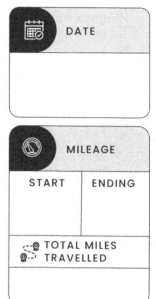

## MILEAGE

| START | ENDING |
|-------|--------|
|       |        |

| TOTAL MILES TRAVELLED | |
|------------------------|--|
|                        |  |

## ACTIVIES PLAN AT TRIP

| | | |
|---|---|---|
| ○ HIKING | ○ SPORTS | ○ |
| ○ FISHING | ○ CYCLING | ○ |
| ○ CANOEING | ○ SITE SEEING | ○ |
| ○ HOTTUB | ○ | ○ |
| ○ BOAT | ○ | ○ |

## WEATHER ON SITE

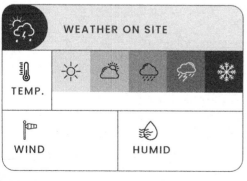

TEMP.

WIND

HUMID

## COST

| TRANSPORT | PACKAGING |
|-----------|-----------|
| FOOD      | OTHER     |

## CAMPGROUND DETAILS

| | |
|---|---|
| LOCATION | DURATION |
| ADDRESS | |
| PHONE | WEB |
| PRICE | RATING ☆☆☆☆☆ |

| ☆☆☆☆☆ | ☆☆☆☆☆ | ☆☆☆☆☆ |
|---|---|---|
| CLEANLINESS | WATER | NOISE |

## TRIP HIGHLIGHTS / MEMORIES

## TRIP LOCATION

### CHECKLIST

### DATE

### MILEAGE

| START | ENDING |
|-------|--------|
|       |        |

| TOTAL MILES TRAVELLED |
|-----------------------|
|                       |

### ACTIVIES PLAN AT TRIP

○ HIKING    ○ SPORTS    ○
○ FISHING   ○ CYCLING   ○
○ CANOEING  ○ SITE SEEING  ○
○ HOTTUB    ○            ○
○ BOAT      ○            ○

### WEATHER ON SITE

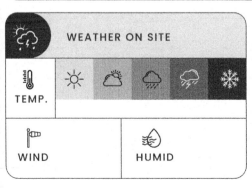

TEMP.

WIND    HUMID

### COST

| TRANSPORT | PACKAGING |
|-----------|-----------|
| FOOD      | OTHER     |

1

## CAMPGROUND DETAILS

| LOCATION | DURATION |
|----------|----------|

| ADDRESS | |
|---------|--|

| PHONE | WEB |
|-------|-----|

| PRICE | RATING ☆☆☆☆☆ |
|-------|----------------|

| ☆☆☆☆☆ | ☆☆☆☆☆ | ☆☆☆☆☆ |
|--------|--------|--------|
| CLEANLINESS | WATER | NOISE |

## TRIP HIGHLIGHTS / MEMORIES

## TRIP LOCATION

### CHECKLIST

### DATE

### MILEAGE

| START | ENDING |
|-------|--------|
|       |        |

TOTAL MILES TRAVELLED

## ACTIVIES PLAN AT TRIP

| | | |
|---|---|---|
| ◯ HIKING | ◯ SPORTS | ◯ |
| ◯ FISHING | ◯ CYCLING | ◯ |
| ◯ CANOEING | ◯ SITE SEEING | ◯ |
| ◯ HOTTUB | ◯ | ◯ |
| ◯ BOAT | ◯ | ◯ |

## WEATHER ON SITE

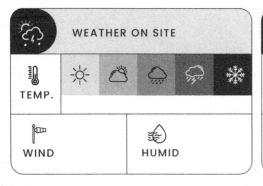

TEMP.

WIND    HUMID

## COST

| TRANSPORT | PACKAGING |
|-----------|-----------|
| FOOD      | OTHER     |

1

## CAMPGROUND DETAILS

| | | | |
|---|---|---|---|
| LOCATION | | DURATION | |
| ADDRESS | | | |
| PHONE | | WEB | |
| PRICE | | RATING ☆☆☆☆☆ | |

| ☆☆☆☆☆ | ☆☆☆☆☆ | ☆☆☆☆☆ |
|---|---|---|
| CLEANLINESS | WATER | NOISE |

## TRIP HIGHLIGHTS / MEMORIES

## TRIP LOCATION

### CHECKLIST

### DATE

### MILEAGE

| START | ENDING |
|-------|--------|
|       |        |

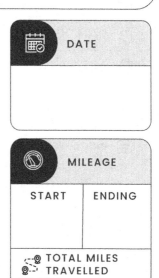 TOTAL MILES TRAVELLED

### ACTIVIES PLAN AT TRIP

- ◯ HIKING
- ◯ FISHING
- ◯ CANOEING
- ◯ HOTTUB
- ◯ BOAT

- ◯ SPORTS
- ◯ CYCLING
- ◯ SITE SEEING
- ◯
- ◯

- ◯
- ◯
- ◯
- ◯
- ◯

### WEATHER ON SITE

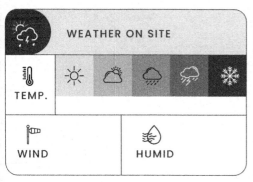

TEMP.

WIND

HUMID

### COST

| TRANSPORT | PACKAGING |
|-----------|-----------|
| FOOD      | OTHER     |

## CAMPGROUND DETAILS

LOCATION

DURATION

ADDRESS

PHONE

WEB

PRICE

RATING ☆☆☆☆☆

☆☆☆☆☆
CLEANLINESS

☆☆☆☆☆
WATER

☆☆☆☆☆
NOISE

## TRIP HIGHLIGHTS / MEMORIES

## TRIP LOCATION

### CHECKLIST

### DATE

### MILEAGE

| START | ENDING |
|-------|--------|
|       |        |

🗺️ TOTAL MILES TRAVELLED

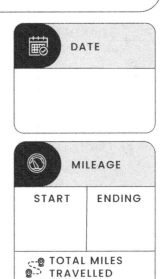

### ACTIVIES PLAN AT TRIP

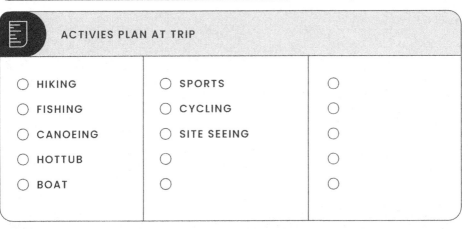

| | | |
|---|---|---|
| ⭘ HIKING | ⭘ SPORTS | ⭘ |
| ⭘ FISHING | ⭘ CYCLING | ⭘ |
| ⭘ CANOEING | ⭘ SITE SEEING | ⭘ |
| ⭘ HOTTUB | ⭘ | ⭘ |
| ⭘ BOAT | ⭘ | ⭘ |

### WEATHER ON SITE

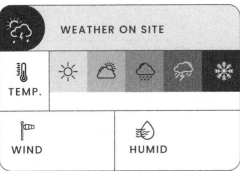

TEMP.

WIND    HUMID

### COST

| TRANSPORT | PACKAGING |
|-----------|-----------|
| FOOD      | OTHER     |

## CAMPGROUND DETAILS

**LOCATION**

**DURATION**

**ADDRESS**

**PHONE**

**WEB**

**PRICE**

**RATING** ☆☆☆☆☆

☆☆☆☆☆
**CLEANLINESS**

☆☆☆☆☆
**WATER**

☆☆☆☆☆
**NOISE**

## TRIP HIGHLIGHTS / MEMORIES

# TRIP LOCATION

## CHECKLIST

## DATE

## MILEAGE

| START | ENDING |
|-------|--------|

TOTAL MILES TRAVELLED

## ACTIVIES PLAN AT TRIP

- ○ HIKING
- ○ FISHING
- ○ CANOEING
- ○ HOTTUB
- ○ BOAT

- ○ SPORTS
- ○ CYCLING
- ○ SITE SEEING
- ○
- ○

- ○
- ○
- ○
- ○
- ○

## WEATHER ON SITE

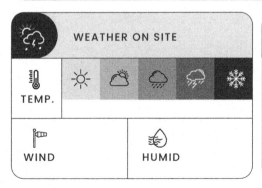

TEMP.

WIND

HUMID

## COST

| TRANSPORT | PACKAGING |
|-----------|-----------|
| FOOD | OTHER |

## CAMPGROUND DETAILS

**LOCATION**

**DURATION**

**ADDRESS**

**PHONE**

**WEB**

**PRICE**

**RATING** ☆☆☆☆☆

☆☆☆☆☆
**CLEANLINESS**

☆☆☆☆☆
**WATER**

☆☆☆☆☆
**NOISE**

## TRIP HIGHLIGHTS / MEMORIES

2

## TRIP LOCATION

### CHECKLIST

### DATE

### MILEAGE

| START | ENDING |
|-------|--------|
|       |        |

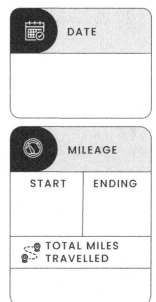 TOTAL MILES TRAVELLED

## ACTIVIES PLAN AT TRIP

| | | |
|---|---|---|
| ○ HIKING | ○ SPORTS | ○ |
| ○ FISHING | ○ CYCLING | ○ |
| ○ CANOEING | ○ SITE SEEING | ○ |
| ○ HOTTUB | ○ | ○ |
| ○ BOAT | ○ | ○ |

## WEATHER ON SITE

| TEMP. | ☀ | ⛅ | 🌧 | ⛈ | ❄ |
|-------|---|---|---|---|---|
| WIND | | HUMID | | | |

## COST

| TRANSPORT | PACKAGING |
|-----------|-----------|
| FOOD | OTHER |

## CAMPGROUND DETAILS

**LOCATION**

**DURATION**

**ADDRESS**

**PHONE**

**WEB**

**PRICE**

**RATING** ☆☆☆☆☆

☆☆☆☆☆
**CLEANLINESS**

☆☆☆☆☆
**WATER**

☆☆☆☆☆
**NOISE**

## TRIP HIGHLIGHTS / MEMORIES

## TRIP LOCATION

### CHECKLIST

### DATE

### MILEAGE

| START | ENDING |
|-------|--------|
|       |        |

TOTAL MILES TRAVELLED

### ACTIVIES PLAN AT TRIP

- ○ HIKING
- ○ FISHING
- ○ CANOEING
- ○ HOTTUB
- ○ BOAT

- ○ SPORTS
- ○ CYCLING
- ○ SITE SEEING
- ○
- ○

- ○
- ○
- ○
- ○
- ○

### WEATHER ON SITE

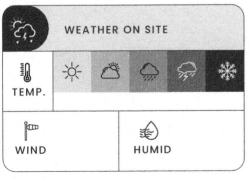

TEMP.

WIND

HUMID

### COST

| TRANSPORT | PACKAGING |
|-----------|-----------|
| FOOD      | OTHER     |

## CAMPGROUND DETAILS

| LOCATION | DURATION |
|----------|----------|
| ADDRESS | |
| PHONE | WEB |
| PRICE | RATING ☆☆☆☆☆ |

☆☆☆☆☆
**CLEANLINESS**

☆☆☆☆☆
**WATER**

☆☆☆☆☆
**NOISE**

## TRIP HIGHLIGHTS / MEMORIES

## TRIP LOCATION

## CHECKLIST

## DATE

## MILEAGE

| START | ENDING |
|-------|--------|
|       |        |

TOTAL MILES TRAVELLED

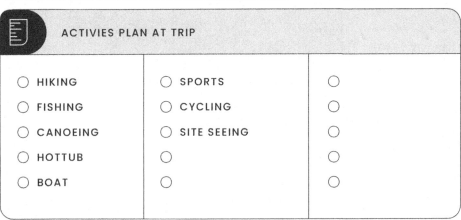

## ACTIVIES PLAN AT TRIP

| ⬡ HIKING | ⬡ SPORTS | ⬡ |
| ⬡ FISHING | ⬡ CYCLING | ⬡ |
| ⬡ CANOEING | ⬡ SITE SEEING | ⬡ |
| ⬡ HOTTUB | ⬡ | ⬡ |
| ⬡ BOAT | ⬡ | ⬡ |

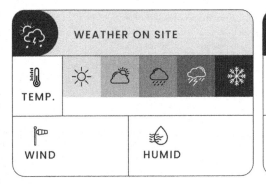

## WEATHER ON SITE

| TEMP. | ☀ | ⛅ | ☔ | ⛈ | ❄ |

| WIND | HUMID |

## COST

| TRANSPORT | PACKAGING |
|-----------|-----------|
| FOOD | OTHER |

## CAMPGROUND DETAILS

| | |
|---|---|
| LOCATION | DURATION |
| ADDRESS | |
| PHONE | WEB |
| PRICE | RATING ☆☆☆☆☆ |

| ☆☆☆☆☆ | ☆☆☆☆☆ | ☆☆☆☆☆ |
|---|---|---|
| CLEANLINESS | WATER | NOISE |

## TRIP HIGHLIGHTS / MEMORIES

## TRIP LOCATION

## CHECKLIST

## DATE

## MILEAGE

| START | ENDING |
|-------|--------|

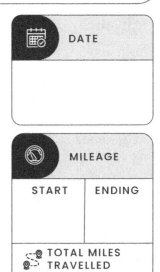 TOTAL MILES TRAVELLED

## ACTIVIES PLAN AT TRIP

- ○ HIKING
- ○ FISHING
- ○ CANOEING
- ○ HOTTUB
- ○ BOAT

- ○ SPORTS
- ○ CYCLING
- ○ SITE SEEING
- ○
- ○

- ○
- ○
- ○
- ○
- ○

## WEATHER ON SITE

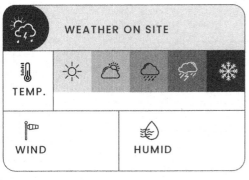

| TEMP. | ☀ | ⛅ | 🌧 | ⛈ | ❄ |
|-------|---|---|---|---|---|

| WIND | HUMID |
|------|-------|

## COST

| TRANSPORT | PACKAGING |
|-----------|-----------|
| FOOD | OTHER |

1

## CAMPGROUND DETAILS

**LOCATION**

**DURATION**

**ADDRESS**

**PHONE**

**WEB**

**PRICE**

**RATING** ☆☆☆☆☆

☆☆☆☆☆
**CLEANLINESS**

☆☆☆☆☆
**WATER**

☆☆☆☆☆
**NOISE**

## TRIP HIGHLIGHTS / MEMORIES

## TRIP LOCATION

## CHECKLIST

## DATE

## MILEAGE

| START | ENDING |
|-------|--------|
|       |        |

TOTAL MILES TRAVELLED

## ACTIVIES PLAN AT TRIP

- ◯ HIKING
- ◯ FISHING
- ◯ CANOEING
- ◯ HOTTUB
- ◯ BOAT

- ◯ SPORTS
- ◯ CYCLING
- ◯ SITE SEEING
- ◯
- ◯

- ◯
- ◯
- ◯
- ◯
- ◯

## WEATHER ON SITE

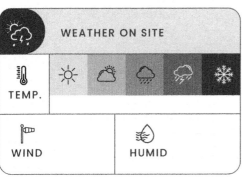

TEMP.

WIND

HUMID

## COST

| TRANSPORT | PACKAGING |
|-----------|-----------|
| FOOD      | OTHER     |

## CAMPGROUND DETAILS

**LOCATION**

**DURATION**

**ADDRESS**

**PHONE**

**WEB**

**PRICE**

**RATING** ☆☆☆☆☆

☆☆☆☆☆
**CLEANLINESS**

☆☆☆☆☆
**WATER**

☆☆☆☆☆
**NOISE**

## TRIP HIGHLIGHTS / MEMORIES

# TRIP LOCATION

## CHECKLIST

## DATE

## MILEAGE

| START | ENDING |
|-------|--------|
|       |        |

| TOTAL MILES TRAVELLED |
|-----------------------|
|                       |

## ACTIVIES PLAN AT TRIP

- ○ HIKING
- ○ FISHING
- ○ CANOEING
- ○ HOTTUB
- ○ BOAT

- ○ SPORTS
- ○ CYCLING
- ○ SITE SEEING
- ○
- ○

- ○
- ○
- ○
- ○
- ○

## WEATHER ON SITE

| TEMP. | ☀ | ⛅ | 🌧 | ⛈ | ❄ |
|-------|---|---|---|---|---|

| WIND | HUMID |
|------|-------|

## COST

| TRANSPORT | PACKAGING |
|-----------|-----------|
| FOOD      | OTHER     |

## CAMPGROUND DETAILS

| LOCATION | DURATION |
|---|---|
| ADDRESS | |
| PHONE | WEB |
| PRICE | RATING ☆☆☆☆☆ |

☆☆☆☆☆
**CLEANLINESS**

☆☆☆☆☆
**WATER**

☆☆☆☆☆
**NOISE**

## TRIP HIGHLIGHTS / MEMORIES

## TRIP LOCATION

### CHECKLIST

### DATE

### MILEAGE

| START | ENDING |
|-------|--------|
|       |        |

TOTAL MILES TRAVELLED

### ACTIVIES PLAN AT TRIP

| | | |
|---|---|---|
| ⭕ HIKING | ⭕ SPORTS | ⭕ |
| ⭕ FISHING | ⭕ CYCLING | ⭕ |
| ⭕ CANOEING | ⭕ SITE SEEING | ⭕ |
| ⭕ HOTTUB | ⭕ | ⭕ |
| ⭕ BOAT | ⭕ | ⭕ |

### WEATHER ON SITE

TEMP.

WIND

HUMID

### COST

| TRANSPORT | PACKAGING |
|-----------|-----------|
| FOOD | OTHER |

## CAMPGROUND DETAILS

| LOCATION | DURATION |
|---|---|
| ADDRESS | |
| PHONE | WEB |
| PRICE | RATING ☆☆☆☆☆ |

☆☆☆☆☆
**CLEANLINESS**

☆☆☆☆☆
**WATER**

☆☆☆☆☆
**NOISE**

## TRIP HIGHLIGHTS / MEMORIES

_____
_____
_____
_____
_____
_____
_____
_____
_____
_____
_____
_____
_____
_____

# TRIP LOCATION

## CHECKLIST

## DATE

## MILEAGE

| START | ENDING |
| --- | --- |
|  |  |

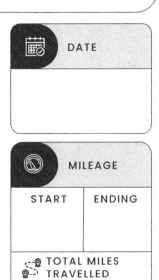 TOTAL MILES TRAVELLED

## ACTIVIES PLAN AT TRIP

- ○ HIKING
- ○ FISHING
- ○ CANOEING
- ○ HOTTUB
- ○ BOAT

- ○ SPORTS
- ○ CYCLING
- ○ SITE SEEING
- ○
- ○

- ○
- ○
- ○
- ○
- ○

## WEATHER ON SITE

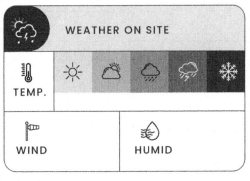

TEMP.

WIND

HUMID

## COST

| TRANSPORT | PACKAGING |
| --- | --- |
| FOOD | OTHER |

## CAMPGROUND DETAILS

**LOCATION**

**DURATION**

**ADDRESS**

**PHONE**

**WEB**

**PRICE**

**RATING** ☆☆☆☆☆

☆☆☆☆☆
CLEANLINESS

☆☆☆☆☆
WATER

☆☆☆☆☆
NOISE

## TRIP HIGHLIGHTS / MEMORIES

**TRIP LOCATION**

**CHECKLIST**

**DATE**

**MILEAGE**

| START | ENDING |
|-------|--------|
|       |        |

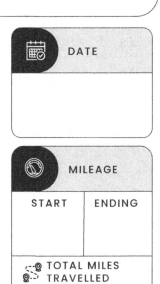

TOTAL MILES TRAVELLED

**ACTIVIES PLAN AT TRIP**

| | | |
|---|---|---|
| ◯ HIKING | ◯ SPORTS | ◯ |
| ◯ FISHING | ◯ CYCLING | ◯ |
| ◯ CANOEING | ◯ SITE SEEING | ◯ |
| ◯ HOTTUB | ◯ | ◯ |
| ◯ BOAT | ◯ | ◯ |

**WEATHER ON SITE**

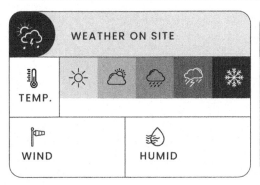

TEMP.

WIND     HUMID

**COST**

| TRANSPORT | PACKAGING |
|-----------|-----------|
| FOOD      | OTHER     |

1

## CAMPGROUND DETAILS

| | |
|---|---|
| LOCATION | DURATION |
| ADDRESS | |
| PHONE | WEB |
| PRICE | RATING ☆☆☆☆☆ |

| CLEANLINESS | WATER | NOISE |
|---|---|---|
| ☆☆☆☆☆ | ☆☆☆☆☆ | ☆☆☆☆☆ |

## TRIP HIGHLIGHTS / MEMORIES

# TRIP LOCATION

## CHECKLIST

## DATE

## MILEAGE

| START | ENDING |
|-------|--------|
|       |        |

TOTAL MILES TRAVELLED

## ACTIVIES PLAN AT TRIP

- ○ HIKING
- ○ FISHING
- ○ CANOEING
- ○ HOTTUB
- ○ BOAT

- ○ SPORTS
- ○ CYCLING
- ○ SITE SEEING
- ○
- ○

- ○
- ○
- ○
- ○
- ○

## WEATHER ON SITE

TEMP.

WIND

HUMID

## COST

| TRANSPORT | PACKAGING |
|-----------|-----------|
| FOOD      | OTHER     |

## CAMPGROUND DETAILS

| | | | |
|---|---|---|---|
| **LOCATION** | | **DURATION** | |
| **ADDRESS** | | | |
| **PHONE** | | **WEB** | |
| **PRICE** | | **RATING** ☆☆☆☆☆ | |

☆☆☆☆☆
**CLEANLINESS**

☆☆☆☆☆
**WATER**

☆☆☆☆☆
**NOISE**

## TRIP HIGHLIGHTS / MEMORIES

## TRIP LOCATION

## CHECKLIST

## DATE

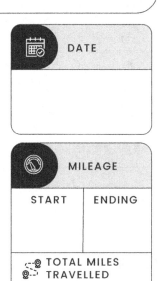

## MILEAGE

| START | ENDING |
|-------|--------|

### TOTAL MILES TRAVELLED

## ACTIVIES PLAN AT TRIP

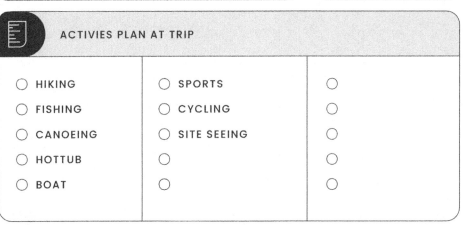

| | | |
|---|---|---|
| ○ HIKING | ○ SPORTS | ○ |
| ○ FISHING | ○ CYCLING | ○ |
| ○ CANOEING | ○ SITE SEEING | ○ |
| ○ HOTTUB | ○ | ○ |
| ○ BOAT | ○ | ○ |

## WEATHER ON SITE

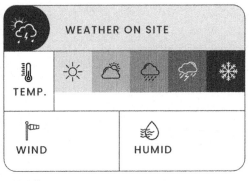

| TEMP. | ☀ ⛅ 🌧 ⛈ ❄ |
|-------|-----------|
| WIND | HUMID |

## COST

| TRANSPORT | PACKAGING |
|-----------|-----------|
| FOOD | OTHER |

## CAMPGROUND DETAILS

| | |
|---|---|
| LOCATION | DURATION |
| ADDRESS | |
| PHONE | WEB |
| PRICE | RATING ☆☆☆☆☆ |

☆☆☆☆☆
**CLEANLINESS**

☆☆☆☆☆
**WATER**

☆☆☆☆☆
**NOISE**

## TRIP HIGHLIGHTS / MEMORIES

# TRIP LOCATION

## CHECKLIST

## DATE

## MILEAGE

| START | ENDING |
|-------|--------|
|       |        |

TOTAL MILES TRAVELLED

## ACTIVIES PLAN AT TRIP

| | | |
|---|---|---|
| ◯ HIKING | ◯ SPORTS | ◯ |
| ◯ FISHING | ◯ CYCLING | ◯ |
| ◯ CANOEING | ◯ SITE SEEING | ◯ |
| ◯ HOTTUB | ◯ | ◯ |
| ◯ BOAT | ◯ | ◯ |

## WEATHER ON SITE

TEMP.

WIND

HUMID

## COST

| TRANSPORT | PACKAGING |
|-----------|-----------|
| FOOD | OTHER |

## CAMPGROUND DETAILS

| | | |
|---|---|---|
| LOCATION | | DURATION |
| ADDRESS | | |
| PHONE | | WEB |
| PRICE | | RATING ☆☆☆☆☆ |

| ☆☆☆☆☆ | ☆☆☆☆☆ | ☆☆☆☆☆ |
|---|---|---|
| CLEANLINESS | WATER | NOISE |

## TRIP HIGHLIGHTS / MEMORIES

## TRIP LOCATION

### CHECKLIST

### DATE

### MILEAGE

| START | ENDING |
|-------|--------|

TOTAL MILES TRAVELLED

### ACTIVIES PLAN AT TRIP

- ○ HIKING
- ○ FISHING
- ○ CANOEING
- ○ HOTTUB
- ○ BOAT

- ○ SPORTS
- ○ CYCLING
- ○ SITE SEEING
- ○
- ○

- ○
- ○
- ○
- ○
- ○

### WEATHER ON SITE

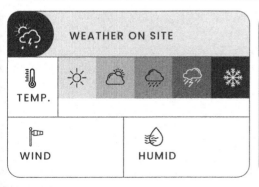

TEMP.

WIND | HUMID

### COST

| TRANSPORT | PACKAGING |
|-----------|-----------|
| FOOD | OTHER |

## CAMPGROUND DETAILS

**LOCATION**

**DURATION**

**ADDRESS**

**PHONE**

**WEB**

**PRICE**

**RATING** ☆☆☆☆☆

☆☆☆☆☆
CLEANLINESS

☆☆☆☆☆
WATER

☆☆☆☆☆
NOISE

## TRIP HIGHLIGHTS / MEMORIES

# TRIP LOCATION

## CHECKLIST

## DATE

## MILEAGE

| START | ENDING |
|-------|--------|
|       |        |

TOTAL MILES TRAVELLED

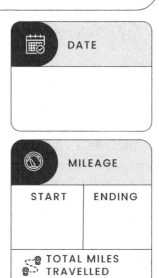

## ACTIVIES PLAN AT TRIP

- ○ HIKING
- ○ FISHING
- ○ CANOEING
- ○ HOTTUB
- ○ BOAT

- ○ SPORTS
- ○ CYCLING
- ○ SITE SEEING
- ○
- ○

- ○
- ○
- ○
- ○
- ○

## WEATHER ON SITE

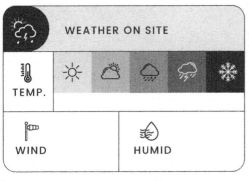

TEMP.

WIND

HUMID

## COST

| TRANSPORT | PACKAGING |
|-----------|-----------|
| FOOD      | OTHER     |

## CAMPGROUND DETAILS

**LOCATION**

**DURATION**

**ADDRESS**

**PHONE**

**WEB**

**PRICE**

**RATING** ☆☆☆☆☆

☆☆☆☆☆
**CLEANLINESS**

☆☆☆☆☆
**WATER**

☆☆☆☆☆
**NOISE**

## TRIP HIGHLIGHTS / MEMORIES

## TRIP LOCATION

### CHECKLIST

### DATE

### MILEAGE

| START | ENDING |
| --- | --- |
| | |

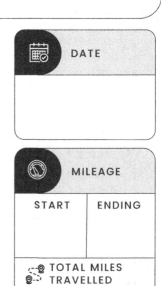 TOTAL MILES TRAVELLED

### ACTIVIES PLAN AT TRIP

- ◯ HIKING
- ◯ FISHING
- ◯ CANOEING
- ◯ HOTTUB
- ◯ BOAT

- ◯ SPORTS
- ◯ CYCLING
- ◯ SITE SEEING
- ◯
- ◯

- ◯
- ◯
- ◯
- ◯
- ◯

### WEATHER ON SITE

| TEMP. | ☀ | ⛅ | ☁ | 🌧 | ❄ |
| --- | --- | --- | --- | --- | --- |
| WIND | | HUMID | | | |

### COST

| TRANSPORT | PACKAGING |
| --- | --- |
| FOOD | OTHER |

1

## CAMPGROUND DETAILS

LOCATION                    DURATION

ADDRESS

PHONE                       WEB

PRICE                       RATING ☆☆☆☆☆

☆☆☆☆☆              ☆☆☆☆☆              ☆☆☆☆☆
CLEANLINESS              WATER                    NOISE

## TRIP HIGHLIGHTS / MEMORIES

## TRIP LOCATION

## CHECKLIST

## DATE

## MILEAGE

| START | ENDING |
|-------|--------|
|       |        |

TOTAL MILES TRAVELLED

## ACTIVIES PLAN AT TRIP

- ○ HIKING
- ○ FISHING
- ○ CANOEING
- ○ HOTTUB
- ○ BOAT

- ○ SPORTS
- ○ CYCLING
- ○ SITE SEEING
- ○
- ○

- ○
- ○
- ○
- ○
- ○

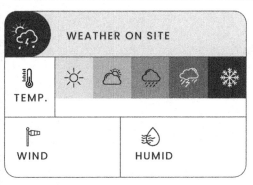

## WEATHER ON SITE

| TEMP. | | | | | |
|-------|--|--|--|--|--|

| WIND | HUMID |
|------|-------|

## COST

| TRANSPORT | PACKAGING |
|-----------|-----------|
| FOOD      | OTHER     |

## CAMPGROUND DETAILS

| LOCATION | DURATION |
|----------|----------|

ADDRESS

| PHONE | WEB |
|-------|-----|

| PRICE | RATING ☆☆☆☆☆ |
|-------|----------------|

| ☆☆☆☆☆ | ☆☆☆☆☆ | ☆☆☆☆☆ |
|--------|--------|--------|
| CLEANLINESS | WATER | NOISE |

## TRIP HIGHLIGHTS / MEMORIES

## TRIP LOCATION

### CHECKLIST

### DATE

### MILEAGE

| START | ENDING |
|-------|--------|
|       |        |

TOTAL MILES TRAVELLED

### ACTIVIES PLAN AT TRIP

- ○ HIKING
- ○ FISHING
- ○ CANOEING
- ○ HOTTUB
- ○ BOAT

- ○ SPORTS
- ○ CYCLING
- ○ SITE SEEING
- ○
- ○

- ○
- ○
- ○
- ○
- ○

### WEATHER ON SITE

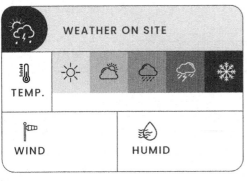

| TEMP. | | | | | |
|-------|--|--|--|--|--|
| WIND | | HUMID | | | |

### COST

| TRANSPORT | PACKAGING |
|-----------|-----------|
| FOOD | OTHER |

## CAMPGROUND DETAILS

**LOCATION**

**DURATION**

**ADDRESS**

**PHONE**

**WEB**

**PRICE**

**RATING** ☆☆☆☆☆

☆☆☆☆☆
**CLEANLINESS**

☆☆☆☆☆
**WATER**

☆☆☆☆☆
**NOISE**

## TRIP HIGHLIGHTS / MEMORIES

**TRIP LOCATION**

**CHECKLIST**

**DATE**

**MILEAGE**

| START | ENDING |
| --- | --- |
| | |

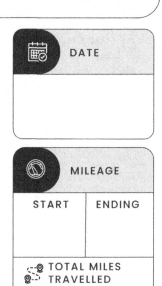

TOTAL MILES TRAVELLED

**ACTIVIES PLAN AT TRIP**

| | | |
| --- | --- | --- |
| ○ HIKING | ○ SPORTS | ○ |
| ○ FISHING | ○ CYCLING | ○ |
| ○ CANOEING | ○ SITE SEEING | ○ |
| ○ HOTTUB | ○ | ○ |
| ○ BOAT | ○ | ○ |

**WEATHER ON SITE**

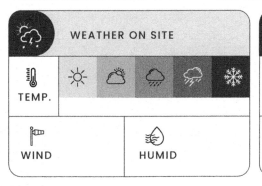

TEMP.

WIND

HUMID

**COST**

| TRANSPORT | PACKAGING |
| --- | --- |
| FOOD | OTHER |

## CAMPGROUND DETAILS

| | |
|---|---|
| LOCATION | DURATION |
| ADDRESS | |
| PHONE | WEB |
| PRICE | RATING ☆☆☆☆☆ |

☆☆☆☆☆
CLEANLINESS

☆☆☆☆☆
WATER

☆☆☆☆☆
NOISE

## TRIP HIGHLIGHTS / MEMORIES

---

---

---

---

---

---

---

---

---

---

---

---

---

## TRIP LOCATION

### CHECKLIST

### DATE

### MILEAGE

| START | ENDING |
|-------|--------|
|       |        |

TOTAL MILES TRAVELLED

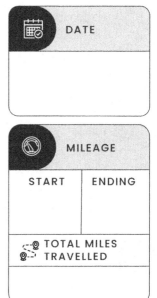

### ACTIVIES PLAN AT TRIP

- ⚪ HIKING
- ⚪ FISHING
- ⚪ CANOEING
- ⚪ HOTTUB
- ⚪ BOAT

- ⚪ SPORTS
- ⚪ CYCLING
- ⚪ SITE SEEING
- ⚪
- ⚪

- ⚪
- ⚪
- ⚪
- ⚪
- ⚪

### WEATHER ON SITE

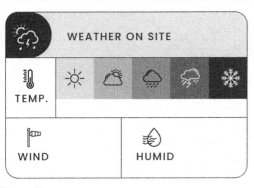

TEMP.

WIND

HUMID

### COST

| TRANSPORT | PACKAGING |
|-----------|-----------|
| FOOD      | OTHER     |

1

## CAMPGROUND DETAILS

LOCATION

DURATION

ADDRESS

PHONE

WEB

PRICE

RATING ☆☆☆☆☆

☆☆☆☆☆
CLEANLINESS

☆☆☆☆☆
WATER

☆☆☆☆☆
NOISE

## TRIP HIGHLIGHTS / MEMORIES

Made in the USA
Monee, IL
11 May 2021